Discover the words for colours.
    to the tune of 'I can sing a rainbow'.

What sports do you love and loathe? Do you play sports? Why? Sketch some pictures with your words.

List the days of the week and months of the year.

First, second, third, fourth, fifth, sixth……..find these out.

Learn the names for kinds of places like the library, chemist, coffee shop, spa, hairdressers and bakery. Draw some symbols for each place.

Describe your bedroom and draw a plan of it. What things are in it?

Jot down numbers 1-20, learn how to recite them in reverse.

Find out how to say your name, your age, and where you are from. Practice whispering and shouting this.

Write a list of things you might buy from a chemist.

Please, thank you, no thank you, I love you and go away. You could rehearse these on a dog or cat.

Things I use in the kitchen….

Numbers 20 - 40. Alternate whispering and shouting the numbers.

How do you like to get around? By car? On a bus? Hot air balloon?... Find some transportation words.

Find out the parts of the face and draw them here.

Do you like fruits? List them here......

Record a new answerphone message, have a message in both languages.

List some breakfast foods and drinks in the style of a menu.

You are at the airport and need to find a taxi to take you to your destination. What questions can help you do this?

She/he/they is/are my/yours. Find these out and create some phrases to talk about friends.

Write down your weekly shopping list and test yourself at the supermarket.

Write the lyrics to head, shoulders, knees, and toes. Perform this song in the shower with actions.

On weeknights I like to...

Learn how to ask for a style of haircut and colour.

List ten things you can't live without. Write sentences that start with 'I can't live without...'

What kind of house do you live in? How many rooms does it have? What are the names of the rooms?

Big, bigger and biggest. Fast, faster and fastest. Clean, cleaner and cleanest. Find out how to talk about comparatives.

What is your favourite TV show? What do you like about it?

Watch a movie with subtitles and make some notes.
What did you like about the movie?

What will you do tomorrow, next week, next month, next year? Draw a timeline. Use the future tense to talk about your plans.

What do you do for work? Where do you work? Is your boss nice or not nice?

Learn parts of the body and draw them here if you like.

Write down some things that are loud and some things that are quiet.

What time is it? Find out quarter past, half past and beyond. Draw lots of clocks for this.

Describe your daily routine, for example 'I get up at 7.30, I eat breakfast at 8.00'.

Where do you go on holiday? What are your top five things to do on holiday?

Write a list of ice cream flavours.

Learn the seasons. Which season do you like and why?

What are you wearing today? Write down some items of clothing.

I don't like Mondays because...Find out some words to describe a situation you don't like.

Find out the names of animals that are great hunters.

My next big trip will be...

I am going skiing. I need to pack my... I need to book a...What is the snow report?

Arrange to meet a friend at a certain time and place.
Confirm your plans by text.

Things I use at work every day.

Before I go to bed I.....Write down the things you do each evening.

Eggs are used in many different types of foods such as....

What do you like about spring?

What makes you sad? Why?

I like to use the sauna, steam room, jacuzzi, and pool. Talk about the spa.

Write down the things that scare you. Include emotions as well as haunted houses.

What drinks hit the spot for you? Find out how to say, 'I like...and I love...'(and bottoms up or cheers)

In very basic steps write and draw how to build a snowman.

What animals live in a forest? Are you scared of them?

Do you use social media? Find some words to talk about which platforms you use and why?

Learn the words for sun, moon, and stars. If you are serious then do the whole solar system!

Describe your siblings. Be nice!

Learn a Christmas carol and write it here. Be sure to practice it in the style of a carol singer that has something to prove.

Write down some names of Zoo animals? Which one do you like? Why?

My favourite shop sells... and I like it because of...

What kind of art do you like?

Look outside your window. What can you see?

More than, fewer than, greater than, lesser than. Describe some objects you have using these words. Start sentences with 'I have/she has/he has'.

Learn the names of fish and shellfish.

Let's go camping! Pack a tent, a sleeping bag, a map....

Can you play a musical instrument? Are you good at it? How long have you played for?

What do you do at Easter? What do you give? Who do you visit?

Learn how to sing happy birthday. Record it and send to a loved one as a voice message on their special day.

What happened in your last dream? In my last dream I....

Things I use in the bathroom....

Visit a museum or art gallery. Find words to give a brief description of what you saw.

I danced, sang, rode, laughed, wondered, smiled, finished....

Write down the names of bakery items and how to order them, for example 'I would like a cookie'. Draw some pictures too.

I want a car/pony/diamond for my birthday. Your wish list starts with...

In an emergency don't panic! Write some phrases below to help.

List some sweet and sour foods.

Find out the words for greetings and write them below. Once you've completed this shout them all loudly!

What makes you laugh? Who makes you laugh until you cry?

Numbers 40- 60. You need to know these!

Its a hot day let's go to the beach. I need...

Binge watch a tv show with subtitles. Make notes on it here. Who was your favourite character?

How is the weather? Draw some pictures for this one.

What did you do last week? Last month? Last year?
Use past tense.

More than one of something. Find out the plurals for words in groups like fruit, vegetables, and clothing.

What would you like for dinner? Draw it, write it, cook it and serve it.

Describe your perfect night at home. My perfect night at home is...

Who are your family members? Who are you closest too?

Learn how to tell your date/spouse/bestie that they are handsome, smart, good at something...

List some things that are hot and some things that are cold.

Find out the basic equation words such as plus, minus, and equals.

It's cold outside, I need some warm clothes. List some winter clothes.

Games I like, games I dislike...

My last text message was......

List down some big things and small things.

The day of the week I like most is...I like that it makes me feel...

Describe your garden or an imaginary garden. I like ponds, trees, purple flowers and wooden gates.

What genre of cinema do you like? Find out some movie genres.

Find out the names of countries and continents. Draw a map.

Learn the words for classroom subjects. Talk about the ones you like and dislike.

Do you have a pet? If not find out how to say your reasons for not having one.

Write the ingredients for something you like to cook or bake.

Go on YouTube and find a cheesy love song. Learn the chorus and practice singing it with your comb or hairbrush as a microphone.

Create a list of either make-up or shaving products.

What are you doing right now? Describe using the present tense.

We are going on a hike. What's the weather like?
What will you take with you?

Write down some savoury foods.

What are your top goals?

I can read, swim, eat, talk, dance, run. I am reading, swimming, eating, talking, dancing, running. Find the verbs and the correct tenses.

My last phone conversation was with my....and we talked about...

Ask for directions to your nearest shopping centre.
Make sure you know your left and right.

Who do you spend your time with the most? Find out how to introduce someone and say how you know them...

Learn how to tell a 'knock-knock' joke and practice getting your intonation correct. Tell it to your neighbour/lover/colleague.

Go for a nature walk and learn how to name the flowers, trees, and birds you see.

Numbers 60 - 100. Find the word for thousand and million.

Find texture words like soft, rough, coarse, smooth....

Write a note of gratitude to someone you hold dear.

Report the weather for today and tomorrow.

At the fairground I like to ride...

Describe your favourite band, movie star or sportsman.

Notes

Notes

Made in the USA
Coppell, TX
23 April 2025